crying
last straw strategies

last straw strategies
99 tips to bring you back from the end of your rope

Crying

Michelle Kennedy

BARRON'S

First edition for the United States, its territories and possessions, and Canada published in 2003 by BARRON'S EDUCATIONAL SERIES, INC. by arrangement with THE IVY PRESS LIMITED

All inquiries should be addressed to:
Barron's Educational Series, Inc.
250 Wireless Boulevard
Hauppauge, New York 11788
www.barronseduc.com

International Standard Book Number
0-7641-2438-2

Library of Congress Catalog Card No.
2002108566

This book was conceived,
designed, and produced by
THE IVY PRESS
The Old Candlemakers
West Street
Lewes
East Sussex BN7 2NZ

Every effort has been taken to ensure that all information in this book is correct. This book is not intended to replace consultation with your doctor, surgeon, or other healthcare professional. The author and publisher disclaim any loss, injury, or damage incurred as a consequence, directly or indirectly, of the use and application of the contents of this book.

Creative Director PETER BRIDGEWATER
Publisher SOPHIE COLLINS
Editorial Director STEVE LUCK
Design Manager TONY SEDDON
Senior Project Editor REBECCA SARACENO
Designer JANE LANAWAY
Illustrator EMMA BROWNJOHN

Printed in China by
Hong Kong Graphics & Printing Ltd.
9 8 7 6 5 4 3 2 1

contents

crying
introduction

When mom and dad bring their new baby home for the first time, they are charged with a major responsibility—make this child happy. So, when baby cries, the first question is, "Why? What can we do?" If only babies could talk then it would not be so difficult to respond to their desires. But, as many parents have discovered, babies *can* talk. We just have to listen. Learning to decipher between the hungry cry and

the tired cry takes time. To help you translate, here are some useful tips from parents who have been in your shoes. The book covers a range of ages, from babies to preschoolers and every tip details which age group is targeted. However, these tips should not be seen as rigid rules. Babies and children are all individual and of course behavior will vary. So treat this age indication as a general guide only.

what's the
problem?

Crying is the first form of baby talk. In the beginning, it is your baby's only way to communicate with you; to let you know whether she is hungry, lonely, tired, wet, uncomfortable, too hot, too cold, or just generally frustrated. Sounds like it is impossible to tell the difference between all these messages? It is, at the outset. But before long you will become an expert at figuring out what your baby needs. I'm assuming you won't need help telling when it's time for a diaper pit-stop, but check out these other diagnostic suggestions.

sleepy?

0–6 months

If your baby is crying before naps or bedtime—or maybe a little earlier or later than your normal schedule—she could just be tired. A lot of traveling, time outside, or

days with lots of other people in the house could mean baby needs an earlier bedtime, while a slower day could cue a later one. Try to tailor sleep times to suit the day's activities.

what's the problem?

hungry?

Even if it seems like you just fed junior, he could still be hungry. Babies go through growth spurts, and the four ounces that satisfied him yesterday might not be nearly enough today. If he stops crying after another feeding, you'll know he was trying to tell you that he was hungry. Babies who are eating solids might also be bored with (or actually not like the taste of) something you've been feeding them. Try to vary the menu a little, mixing and matching flavors, and introducing some new taste sensations. You can add bananas to plain rice cereal, or switch to sweet potatoes instead of peas. Bland doesn't have to mean boring!

what's the problem?
bored?

I know it seems like it should be fun for baby to watch you from her infant seat while you fold the laundry, but let's face it—even a two-month-old needs more stimulation than that sometimes. Keep baby active. Let her know the ceiling isn't the only thing to look at in the house.

what's the problem?

overstimulated?

On the flip side, sometimes it is just all too much. Maybe the TV is going, big brother is playing with his walkie talkies, and the mobile over the crib is wreaking havoc with baby's psyche. Put yourself in baby's place for a minute. Aren't there times when you just want to yell "Be quiet!" (or something a little more, shall we say, edgy?) at the top of your lungs? I know I do. Well, if the noise level is giving you a headache, sometimes baby feels the same way. Calm things down a bit. Take baby to a quieter room and let him focus on one thing at a time. Keep him company, talking or singing in a gentle voice for a couple of minutes, and his mood—and yours—will probably improve.

needs to suck?

0–6 months

Sometimes, a baby just has to do it (especially when teething). Sucking is rhythmic, it's comforting, it's calming. If baby doesn't want to eat, offer her a pacifier, one of her thumbs, or one of your knuckles instead.

what's the problem?

lonesome?

All of us feel the need to be held close from time to time. It's said to bring back the feeling of security we experienced when we were still in our mother's womb. It's no shocker, then, that some babies like to feel warmth and a heartbeat on a regular basis. Just pick him up and hold him close, or lie on the floor or couch with him on your chest, so that your heartbeats match.

what's the problem?
colicky?

If baby cries inconsolably every night, often around dinner time, for a few hours, and is unsatisfied by a feeding or a hug or being carried around or any other remedy you can think of, the crying may be caused by colic. How do you know if your baby is colicky? You can identify colic by the hard stomach, rigid legs, and red face of the sufferer. Nobody is sure what causes colic—some people say that colicky babies are gassy; others say they are supersensitive to everything around them. One thing we do know for sure is that it only lasts for a few months. For advice on how to help ease the discomfort of colic, *see pages 23–33*.

what's the problem?

needs to burp?

Babies swallow air, and then they suffer from gas pains, just like anyone else. You can help to prevent this by holding your baby upright as much as possible during feeding and burping. Also, check the nipple hole. The right-size nipple hole on a bottle will also reduce air intake. (If you're breast-feeding, then you have the perfectly sized hole already—and if you didn't, what could you do anyway?) Burp baby regularly during feedings in order to expel swallowed air. Applying light pressure to the baby's abdomen (by laying her across your lap, tummy down, or upright against your shoulder) while patting or rubbing her back also works well.

uncomfortable?

Always double-check to make sure that cries are not a

genuine protest about being too hot, too cold, caught up in

something, or plunked down inadvertently on a spiky toy,

like a plastic brick.

what's the problem?

just crying?

Studies have shown that four out of five babies have daily crying sessions lasting from 15 minutes to an hour for no apparent reason. These crying jags usually occur in the evening, which also tends to be the busiest time of the day at home. There may be a lot of noise and activity as the rest of the family arrives and prepares to settle down for the evening. For the baby it could be the end of a tiring day,

taking in new sights, sounds, and smells. After the sensory overload, some babies like to relax by having a good cry—some moms might want to as well. Keep a log of the crying times for a week, to see if they occur at a regular time each day. If so, when it's time for the daily outburst, you can put your baby in her crib for her howling session, safe in the knowledge that there is nothing really wrong.

what's the problem?

sad baby?

Babies have different temperaments, just as grown-ups do. To some degree, it's the luck of the draw whether you have a baby who fusses, is irritable and easily upset, or one who is easy-going. You may even get one of each in the same family. So despite all your best efforts, your baby might just cry more than others do. But don't despair—his crying stage won't last forever. In the meantime, if your baby's crying is getting you down, it is important to give yourself a break—baby can sense your tension and that might make him feel worse. This is not to say that your feelings *cause* the crying, but without your knowing it, they could possibly be a factor in perpetuating it.

Try to arrange for someone to help out for a few hours—or even a few minutes—so you can treat yourself to some guilt-free personal time. You'll probably find the little piece of extra time you get can make all the difference.

dealing with colic

Some babies have it all of the time. All babies have it some of the time, but nobody knows what causes it. Until it goes away (at around four months of age), there are a number of tricks that can help you through it. Here is a range of cures that have worked for some babies, some of the time.

the colic baby

0-6 months

This is a tip I thought I invented until I met many other moms and dads who had also "invented" this same baby hold. Hold your baby with her head in the crook of your arm (at the elbow) and with your hand grabbing her diaper (or vice versa, with her head in your hand and her bottom toward your elbow). The pressure of her stomach on your forearm will relieve her gas pains. It's also a great alternative if you have a sore bicep, and the baby seems to like it too!

dealing with colic

check your diet

Are you breast-feeding? Eat anything particularly spicy lately? Check your diet for the last couple of days. Whatever you eat passes through to the breast milk that you're feeding to your baby. If you ate anything out of the ordinary or in more abundance than usual, it's possible that baby doesn't like it much. Caffeine, chocolate, chili . . . all of these can put a rumbly in little one's tummy. Some foods that you eat may end up giving your baby gas—like cabbage or onions. Others, like garlic, have strong flavors that your baby might simply not like. It may also be worth cutting down on your own consumption of dairy products, since some babies are very sensitive to cow's milk in the first few months.

white noise

0–6 months

It sounds silly that the noise we so abhor as adults could actually comfort a baby, but give it a try. Static on the radio or television, the vacuum cleaner, the hair dryer—they all make that awful noise but for some reason, it can soothe a cranky baby right to sleep.

dealing with colic

time out

Some people believe that colic is not a result of physical discomfort, but rather of baby's sensitivity to her surroundings. Take some time out for peace and quiet. Shut off the TV, radio, and the more intense lights. Lay baby on your chest and let her hear the rhythm of your heart and the evenness of your breathing.

dealing with colic
baby formulas

Sometimes that special formula you carefully selected just doesn't quite hit the spot. It might fill your little one up all right, but it might also be making him a little queasy or even causing a mild allergic reaction. Keep a journal for a week and take note of how baby is reacting. It is also possible (although rare) that baby is lactose-intolerant, particularly if there is a family history of this, or if he suffers from eczema or other allergies. In that case, a soy-based formula could be better than one based on cow's milk. Consult with your pediatrician if baby seems to be having real issues with formula and always check first before switching to a new brand.

dealing with colic

massage

Who doesn't love a massage? A little baby oil and a slow rub-down can turn any baby into, well . . . a baby. A gentle rub on the tummy could ease gas pain. Invest in one of the many books available on infant massage techniques, or see if there is a local class you can attend.

the dryer

0–6 months

I don't know what it was about my clothes dryer that was so attractive to my babies, but if it was running, then they were really happy if they were on top of it. I should have installed a TV in the laundry room, considering the amount of time I spent in there. I would place baby in his car seat, put in yet another load of laundry (the dryer never had to run empty, that's for sure!), and I would sit on the washing machine reading a book or a magazine, with baby next to me. It wasn't the most comfortable room in the house, but it was the most peaceful one. But before you try this, make sure the car seat is firmly secured—the same motion that can make babies happy can also inch them over the edge, so *don't* leave your baby unattended for a second.

dealing with colic

the baby swing

The best $10 I ever spent at a yard sale was on a baby swing. A friend of mine once showed me her brand-new one that was "whisper quiet." It was beautiful, but her baby wasn't crazy about it, and she couldn't figure out why. She put her colicky baby in my yard-sale swing that made the clackety-clack noise, and her baby fell right asleep! Something about that motion, accompanied by a rhythmic clacking, can put babies right out. Used or new, a baby swing is a great investment. They practically guarantee some peace and quiet during the day. And it's easy to track them down secondhand, since you only use them for a few months. If using secondhand, make sure it's in good condition with a safety strap.

ceiling fans

0–6 months

You're not ever going to get me to understand why babies like these things, but believe me, take any crying baby into your local home improvement or lighting fixture store, and you will immediately have a mesmerized child (assuming she is not hungry). The whirling fans and differently colored lights will keep baby's eyes and brain busy for as long as you need (well, almost).

dealing with colic

exercise with baby

No, don't try to make her do little baby jumping jacks—and I don't mean for you to go and sign up for aerobics classes either. Just lie on your back on the floor, bring your knees to your chest, and place baby, tummy down, on your shins. Brace her shoulders with your forearms, or just hold them lightly but securely, then bounce your legs up and down gently. Make sure that baby stays in contact with your legs the whole time (as your little one gets older, a more vigorous style of bouncing is sure to please, but it's better to start slowly). The pressure on her stomach, combined with the gentle bouncing motion, can soothe baby, for a little while at least. And you'll feel good that you've worked out.

exercise the baby

0–6 months

This one is just for him. Lay baby on his back on the floor, and, holding him by the ankles, move his legs in a gentle, bicycling action. This motion can help him get rid of gas and can also help to relieve constipation. There are other exercises you can try to gently compress baby's abdomen. I liked to vary the regime sometimes by reaching baby's arm to the opposite leg, and so on.

teething

Consider a toothache. Now do you blame your baby for howling? The discomfort starts a few months before the first tooth even appears. You can be pretty sure her grumpiness is caused by teething pains if she's drooling a lot and biting on anything she can find. Try out these ways to ease sore little gums, and thank your lucky stars you can't remember how it felt.

silver cool gums!

Not born with a silver spoon in his mouth? Well, if he's cutting those first teeth—give him one! A silver spoon cooled briefly in the freezer can help baby with those nasty new incisors. Silver retains cold longer than some other teethers, and it isn't a choking hazard. Just don't leave him alone with it, because a quick turn of the spoon to the handle end, and he could make himself gag.

happy and clean

Boil and then freeze a rolled-up washcloth—these are easy for baby to handle and easy for mom to store (we always have washcloths to hand), but make sure you prepare more than one because they don't stay frozen long. One big plus of washcloths is that they help soak up the buckets of drool that are an inevitable by-product of teething.

kitchen magic

teething

6–12 months

Rub lemon juice on the gums. It acts as an astringent to irritated gum tissue and brings some relief. Babies don't seem to mind the sour taste. In fact, children naturally enjoy sour things. That's why kids are always after the green apples in the garden. You can also cut a wedge of lemon and give that to baby to gnaw on. Make sure that you remove all the seeds first, because they are a choking hazard; look for unwaxed lemons, or scrub the peel first to get rid of any substances used to coat it. Obviously, you have to keep your eye on the baby when he is chewing or sucking on anything.

go italian

You know the hard, Italian cookies called "biscotti" (or sometimes known as "ossi dei morti" meaning, bones of the dead) that you like to dunk in your cappuccino? Teething babies like them, too.

If you want to make your own, there's a great recipe at *www.cookierecipe.com*.

"bagels aren't just for eating, mom!"

teething

6-12 months

Freeze that bagel and let baby gnaw herself silly. The cool feels good, and the bagel gives her something to chew on without eating plastic. Bagels are a great solution for a baby who has already cut a tooth or two, because she is unlikely to choke on any pieces she manages to bite off. (A baby with teeth might puncture a soft gel-filled teething ring and possibly ingest the the icky contents inside.) For other edible remedies for younger teethers who haven't got any teeth yet, you can also try freezing the fat end of a peeled carrot or a banana. With any of the food you try, be extremely careful. Make sure baby is sitting upright and keep your eyes on her the whole time.

teething
pressure point

Acupressure is believed to be the forerunner of acupuncture and has many similarities. Acupressure is a system of massage designed to enhance the circulation of vital energy throughout the body in order to restore harmony and good health. Basically, it's acupuncture without the puncture. You can use gentle thumb or index-finger pressure on various points on the body with sometimes

spectacular results. The acupressure point for teething (as well as toothaches and migraines) is on the back of the hand in the web between thumb and index finger. Press firmly but gently with your thumb and rotate slightly. Another one to try in order to stimulate energy and to soothe baby's colic and digestive problems, first find the point about three inches below the knee on the outside of the leg. Press deeply with your thumb for about five minutes. For painful conditions, these treatments can be repeated two or three times every hour. If this works for you and you want to learn more, check out *page 126* for some recommended reading about acupressure.

teething

go natural

If you tried the drugstore gels and they don't work, or you want a more organic approach, look at alternative remedies. Before administering any herbal products to children, however, consult with a knowledgeable and experienced healthcare provider who can give you information about age-appropriate dosages and precautions. Even if the remedy is a natural one (homeopathy treats "like with like"), it is still essential to check it out before using it on your baby. One popular herbal remedy to help relieve teething pain is a dab of clove oil. This may be rubbed on the gums of a teething infant using just your own clean fingers. A very good, fast-

acting homeopathic remedy for teething babies is Chammomilla 12c. A few drops under the tongue will work wonders. If you are still breast-feeding, the Bach Flower Remedy "Rescue Remedy" (easily available at health food stores) will help when used as directed and will not harm baby.

keep them clean

Start young—brush those new
pearly whites as soon as they
appear, to get you and
your baby in the habit
from the beginning. The
action of cleaning can
help soothe the pain,
giving two benefits at
the same time. You can
easily clean baby's new teeth with a wet (clean)
washcloth or gauze. Rubber-finger toothbrushy things are
also available, if you are that way inclined.

no appetite?

teething

6-12 months

Is your baby not eating the way she used to? Teething could be the reason. Although baby makes it clear that she wants something in her mouth, she seems to lose her appetite as soon as she starts to suck or eat. This is because the action of sucking or compressing the gums could make her teething pains worse. Then she gets hungrier and this makes her grumpier and more uncomfortable. Try giving your baby a gum massage before mealtimes, nursing, or the bottle. Sometimes this will soothe enough to get her to start feeding again. Missing a couple of meals is not a disaster, but if she continues to say no for a day or so, you must contact your pediatrician.

gripewater

Known for its usefulness in relieving colic, gripewater is also very effective for teething. It is made from ginger, fennel, sodium bicarbonate, fructose, and water. Ginger and fennel can help solve digestive problems—ginger relieves nausea, and fennel is good for hiccups and gas. Although gripewater won't eliminate teething pains, it can help out with the tummy upset that often accompanies it. It's a bit tricky to make, but easy to find on line at *www.babys-bliss.com* or at most natural food stores.

back to basics

teething

6-12 months

Moms everywhere wanted me to include this little tip. Sometimes, in our efforts to avoid giving our babies anything but natural remedies, we forget about things like acetaminophen and ibuprofen. (Asprin should never be given to a baby because of the risk of Reyes Syndrome— a disease that attacks the body's organs.) A dose before bedtime can give both baby and parents alike a welcome rest. Don't give any medicine to babies under six months old without a doctor's approval, make sure you give the dose appropriate to baby's age, and don't overuse it.

diaper
wars

Is changing time a pain in the butt? A wriggly baby and a frustrated mom or dad makes for a messy combination. There isn't a parent in the world who honestly enjoys changing diapers; and no baby goes along willingly with being changed. But help is at hand—smooth away the tears with these suggestions.

a squirming whiner

0–12 months

Do you have a squirming whiner on your hands? Perhaps your baby simply doesn't like heights. Ditch the changing table, get a soft, colorful beach towel, and change baby on the floor. Put all the supplies into an easy-to-carry basket, and you have a portable changing station. The towel folds up nicely and can be stored under a side table in the living room to allow quick and easy changes.

cotton buds

0–12 months

cold comfort

Those baby wipes can be chilly and are sure to give baby an unpleasant surprise, which, more often than not, will lead to a nice, long cry. Warm up the wipes by placing the container near a radiator or on a sunny windowsill.

wipe out

0–12 months

Don't use commercial baby wipes if your baby's skin is easily irritated—and definitely steer clear of any that contain alcohol. Save them all for sticky fingers and carrot-laden faces. Instead, use warm water and a soft washcloth to cleanse baby's bottom. Buy a package of washcloths dedicated just for this purpose if you feel kind of squeamish about contaminating the rest of the laundry. If baby is particularly messy, a quick dip in the tub may be an easier way to get that little bottom clean. Make sure you dry him thoroughly, either with a soft, clean cloth or just by allowing him to air-dry, before you put on the fresh diaper.

0–12 months

go commando

There's nothing like diaper rash to put baby in a positively foul mood. If he isn't moving a lot yet, put him on his tummy on a blanket on the floor, with an absorbent towel underneath, and let him go commando for a little while. If he is mobile, well, keep a sponge and some disinfectant ready and waiting! Fresh air is a cheap and effective remedy for diaper rash.

let the sun shine

One of the best ways to help clear up diaper rash (or psoriasis) is to put baby on her tummy in the light from a sunny window. This is best done in the early morning or late afternoon when the sun's rays aren't so intense. Dress baby in light-colored clothing to protect unaffected skin and use 30 plus paba-free sunscreen (but keep baby's bottom free from cream). Don't leave her there for too long at a time (some pediatricians recommend 15 minutes or so) and periodically check that she is happy. Just as the sun "bleaches" cloth diapers as they dry, killing the embedded bacteria, so will the sun eliminate the bacteria that is causing the diaper rash. Bacteria love a warm, moist environment (i.e. a diaper) and the sun is their worst enemy.

diaper wars

change brands

Diaper rash still won't clear up? Try switching diaper brands. If you're using disposables and changing brands doesn't help, consider switching to cloth diapers, at least for a little while. If you're already using cloth diapers, change your brand of laundry soap. There are products on the market that are specially formulated to be gentle on a baby's skin. It's also worth cutting out the fabric softener, which does not rinse clean and leaves behind substances that can irritate baby's skin. Alternatively, you can clean the diapers by soaking them either in one of the diaper rinses on the market or in a mixture of vinegar and hot water followed by a hot-water rinse.

don't wipe!

Use a spray bottle full of two cups of warm water and two tablespoons of baking soda to disinfect and clean baby's bottom—then gently pat dry. This natural combination means you don't have to rush out and buy expensive items. Just go into the kitchen and prepare the warm spray. Then squirt at baby's bottom. A creative kind of baby bidet, if you will.

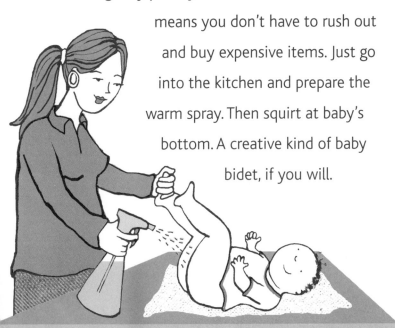

entertainment
central

Hang a mirror on the wall by the changing table—babies love to try to figure out who that very cute person on the other side is. Or have a small set of toys and little board books at the ready. There's nothing like a "Where did this come from?" to distract a baby long enough to get a diaper under her! Reserve these just for diaper changes, so that they maintain their novelty value a little longer. A word of advice, though. Try to figure out a way to secure toys to the changing table, so that when baby throws them over the side—as he will, over and over and over again—it is easy to pull them back up without leaving him unattended. Toys designed to be attached to strollers are a good bet.

music soothes
the savage . . .

Well, you get the idea. For almost any crying jag, a little silly music can do wonders. Add a little goofy dancing (on your part) to the act, and you could have baby laughing before she has time to cry. Just don't forget to get that diaper on before you get your groove on!

mobiles

Hang one of the 30 mobiles you received at the baby shower over the changing table. If you didn't receive more than one, make your own out of a couple of coat hangers and some favorite photos or brightly colored pictures from a magazine. Position it right above baby's face (but not too close for comfort)—if it's over to one side, baby will squirm around to try to get a better view. For newborns, high-contrast, black-and-white images never fail to captivate, and all babies are attracted to pictures of faces. Remember to change your display often so that baby does not become bored with your selection.

remote control

Babies love electronics. (Well, who programs the video chez-vous?) Grab the remote (ok, one of the remotes) or a calculator and let baby press the buttons while you change away. The only danger is that it will be pretty hard to regain control over the remote once the diaper is done! To make matters a little easier for all concerned, give baby an old remote or calculator, without batteries (save the lesson in electricity for another time!). This way, if she drools on it, you won't panic.

cotton wool

where does it
hurt?

Babies cry for many reasons. The most distressing (for you) and fretful one is if they're sick. If your baby is crying more than usual or appears more irritable, and your usual repertoire of calming and comforting tricks simply doesn't work, you could have a sick baby on your hands. Here's some advice on coping with illness.

any other
diagnostic clues?

0–12 months

Trust your instincts. If baby doesn't sound or look right to you, well, you should know. Even if you don't want to bug the doctor—do it anyway. If they signed up to be baby doctors, then they already know what they're getting into. When you do call the doctor, have essential information at the ready, including weight, any medications baby has taken or is taking, any allergies, his temperature, etc. (*see page 127* for further diagnostic clues).

where does it hurt?

MD tips

Bring special treats along for trips to the doctor to keep baby occupied while you wait, and to cheer baby up after treatment. One mom suggests making appointments as early in the day as possible, so that the whole day isn't ruined because of her anxiety over a dreaded shot.

it isn't crying but ... 6 months–4 years

Hiccups are almost as bad, especially when the little one can't stop them for himself. Some babies hiccup a lot, starting when they are still in the womb, others not very much. In newborns hiccups occur for no reason in particular. With older children, they often come on after a long spell of laughter. Usually they clear up on their own. Otherwise a nice drink of water may just do the trick. If this doesn't help after a reasonable amount of time, try gently plugging baby's ears with your fingers for about 20 seconds. Make some funny faces as you are holding their ears. Strange but true—another remedy is to tickle the roof of baby's mouth with a clean cotton swab.

where does it hurt?

holding patterns

If it's nervousness over the doctor that's causing baby's crying and not a physical problem, hold her as much as possible while she's being poked and prodded, offering comfort and reassurance. Some babies are determined wrigglers and won't hold still even for medical treatment, such as shots or stitches. If your baby is one of these, don't be afraid to hold her tightly—better to squeeze her a bit and make you both uncomfortable than to have to give a shot over again! If you're the anxious one—don't be embarrassed, plenty of adults get jittery at the thought of seeing the doctor—holding baby will help you to control your own nerves.

a pain in the ear   6 months–4 years

s baby pulling at her ear? Is she
lying on one side? An earache
could be the culprit so first go to
your doctor for diagnosis. If this
is the case and the doctor
approves it, when baby is
back at home, you could
try to ease the pain of a
minor earache with a few
drops of warm olive oil
using an eyedropper. A hairdryer held at a distance on low
can relieve ear pain with its dry heat. Hot water bottles
wrapped in towels make great pillows for earache sufferers.
However, a head-banging earache usually requires over-the-
counter pain medicine if approved by your doctor.

1-4 years

peas for a bruise?

You bet—or corn, carrots, or whatever else you have in your freezer. When you need ice for a skinned knee or other "boo-boo," use a bag of frozen veggies instead of ice cubes (remember to place a cloth between the frozen bag and baby's skin to avoid ice burns).

Because of the small size of the contents, the plastic bag wraps around a knee or lays on top of a forehead very nicely. Just remember to put them back in the freezer before they thaw completely!

crazy liquids

Doctors are always telling us to push fluids. Dehydration can turn a cranky baby even crankier, but how do you get him to drink when he doesn't want to? The simple and determined answer is: Try everything! Moms from all over suggest using crazy straws, popsicles, sippy cups—whatever floats baby's boat (so to speak) that day. Some foods, like soup or juicy fruits, also have a high fluid content. Even if baby won't take much at any one time, keep offering drinks throughout the day. And use all your ingenuity to get that liquid in. One dad got his particularly picky sick one to drink just by putting juice in his travel coffee mug. All the little guy wanted to do was pretend he was dad for the day, sipping his "coffee" and lying on the couch watching TV.

1-4 years

got milk?

No! Not if your kid is stuffed up with a cold. No cheese, yogurt, milk, or ice cream while he's congested. Dairy products can actually add time to the length of a cold or make the symptoms worse, by thickening the mucus. So when you're pushing fluids, offer water or fruit juices instead—juices have the added bonus of upping baby's vitamin C consumption. If you're a little bit worried about adequate calcium intake for those few days, give him a multivitamin with extra calcium or offer orange juice fortified with calcium.

a pox on your house   0-4 years

When one family member gets chicken pox—you all get it. And we all got it good—four kids and one husband covered with spots at the same time. I have four words for you: vinegar, baking soda, oatmeal. Blend a cup of oatmeal, dump it in the tub with a quarter cup of vinegar and baking soda. The kids will love watching the baking soda and vinegar fizz. Use cool water to take the itch away.

6 months–4 years

conjunctivitis

Even the name is icky. It's pink eye and it's just gross. And a crying baby will make it even worse! Go straight to the doctor for diagnosis. You will get medication from the doctor, but to relieve the itchy and sometimes painful symptoms, try potatoes. I know, I know, it sounds silly. But grate some potato into a paper towel and place over the affected eye. Something in the potato draws the infection out. Another commonplace item of food that is also great for relieving the itch and swelling is the plain and ordinary cucumber. Yes, make your child a spa in your living room by putting cucumber slices over his eyes, and getting him to recline and relax. Read a story while these remedies are on to prevent any anxiety (or boredom) your child may feel. Alternatively, make the situation into some kind of game. You could play "Guess what this smell is?", or "What does this feel like?". If your child is too young to sit still then try squeezing the juice into a paper towel and wiping gently over the eyes every 15 minutes or so.

fat lips

1-4 years

My daughter's first birthday picture is a beautiful one. Her hair is clean and curly, she is wearing the cutest dress ever, the cake is perfect, and . . . she has a huge, fat lip, which she gave herself after chasing one of our cats. When it happened,

she refused to let me put an ice pack on it, so her lip grew! I later learned that a great way to prevent this would have been to offer her a frozen juice pop instead. The ice in the pop will ease the swelling and she gets a treat in the bargain!

bugs in the ear . . .

. . . beans up the nose, whatever. Oh, the things we have to do when we have children. Don't go after it with an instrument of any kind. With a bug in the ear, take the child to a dark room (after calming him down) and look for it with a flashlight. Most bugs will be attracted to the light and (if still alive) they will come right out. If the bug is alive but won't come out, use an eyedropper with a few drops of rubbing alcohol to kill it and then mineral (or olive) oil to gently flood the ear. A bean (or other charming item) up the nose should come out with one good blow out of the nostril (while holding the other nostril closed, of course). In either case, bug or bean, let a doctor remove it with an instrument if it doesn't come right out on its own.

whimpering
babes

Persistent low-level whimpering can be just as nerve-jangling as full-out screaming. Your baby may not be howling, but he's not happy, so neither of you can settle down. Whining doesn't demand desperate measures, and there are many little tricks that can help out. Try these ideas to turn the frowns upside down.

soothing tunes

0–12 months

If the whine level goes up at nap or sleep time, try playing music (CD or cassette—but if you are a flute virtuoso, play live.) Choose something you like, because once baby associates that music with relaxation, you may be hearing a lot of it. Keep the noise down—don't pump up the volume to match the crying level.

Most babies usually quiet down and begin to relax within 15 to 20 minutes of the first track.

whimpering babes

water cure

Take a warm bath with baby, or try bringing her in the shower with you (just make sure you have a good grip or don't mind getting the baby sling wet) if you prefer. Go for a swim if you have access to an indoor pool or other water source. Or simply try running the water—sometimes just the sound will soothe a whiny babe.

whimpering babes
ignore it

I know, it sounds awful. But it's possible that a whimpering baby is only trying to settle down. Lay him in a nice, quiet, calm place without distractions and let him be for a bit. It's quite possible that he will either fall asleep or become interested in his toes or the shadows on the wall and cheer himself up. On the other hand, if the growling turns to howling, then you'll know that there is something really wrong. It's important for baby to learn to amuse himself once in a while. This is a life skill that will always serve him well. And it's one that you'll appreciate, too. Once baby can entertain himself, you will start to get a little time to yourself, to clean up—or to put your feet up!

whimpering babes
unexpected elements

Not wet? Not sleepy? Not hungry? Look for something
unusual—a diaper tape cutting into tummy, or a pin—ouch!
One dad says he stripped baby down only to find a thread
wound tightly around her toe. That'll make anyone cranky!

foot loose

0–12 months

If your baby wears all-in-one outfits with feet, check that her tootsies have not grown overnight (they do, you know) and are cramped inside the little pockets. It might be time to cut the feet off every all-in-one, to prevent painful tightness higher up. It's also important to check socks and booties on a regular basis. To ensure a comfortable fit, there should be a thumb's width of room between the top of baby's longest toe and the end of the sock or bootie. Babies experience several growth spurts in their first year. You'll know something is going on because she seems to be constantly hungry and you feel like you are constantly feeding, so keep your eyes on her feet!

whimpering babes

wrap it up

For very young babies, swaddling can be a great stress reliever. The added tightness around their bodies is comforting. To swaddle: lay the receiving blanket down so that one of the corners is pointing toward you. Lay baby with his head in one corner of the blanket. Wrap one corner (right or left) over baby and tuck it under him. Bring the bottom corner up over his legs and tuck into the just-folded side and then bring the other side over and tuck into the fold. There! A bundle of joy. Depending on age, baby may prefer hands either in or out. Smaller babies, still scared of their own hands (at least it looks that way, doesn't it?) will want them inside.

turn around

0–12 months

Some baby slings come with the
option to face baby outward. Maybe
she's tired of looking at your neck!
So for a welcome change, let her see
where you're going and you'll be
surprised at how quickly the
whining stops. If your sling
doesn't face out, sometimes you
can modify it by folding down the
back support—if anything just as a
temporary measure until you can
purchase or borrow a new one!

sensory experiences

Your baby may be bored. Try some safe new sensations. Gently rub baby's arms with different fabrics: satin, wool, and terry cloth are good fabrics to start with. Give her an opportunity to experience different smells. Take her outside and smell a

flower; smell a freshly cut orange. But be careful not to overstimulate your baby. Watch for signs that she is getting tired of the new game.

whimpering babes
game plan
0-12 months

Baby's first game—"Where is it?" Let your baby see you hide an object under a blanket or a rug and then ask, "Where is it?" Once she becomes an expert at finding a single item, help lengthen her attention span by hiding two or three things at a time. If you're in a confined place, like a waiting room, a car, or an airplane, hide yourself. "Peekaboo," that old standbye, rarely fails to please. Not only are these games a lot of fun but they also teach baby an important lesson—even if she can't see something for a moment, it will come back. Coming to terms with this concept (known as object permanence) will help baby to cope with your own absences.

whimpering babes

find your nose

Your baby loves all of her many body parts, and pointing them out can be a real adventure. At first, you'll have to help out. Ask, "Where is your nose?" or "Where are your toes?" and help baby to point out her own as well as yours. As she gets older, she'll be able to join in, grabbing your nose (and probably squeezing it tight), and reaching for her own toes. This silly game will help her develop both language skills and coordination. Watch for her excitement as she points to the right place for the first time. It's one of those unforgettable moments.

jack in the box

6-12 months

This popular game helps to reinforce the idea that surprises can be fun. Make a fist with both hands and tuck your thumb under the fingers. "Jack in the box sits so still; Won't you come out?; Yes, I will!" On the words, "Yes I will," pop up your thumbs. Help your child make a fist and show him how to pop up his thumb. You can also play this game by crouching down and jumping up, giving yourself a spontaneous aerobic workout.

moving attractions

Many a crying baby has been soothed by movement. This is why moms and dads have been known to stick an inconsolable baby in the car or the stroller for late-night excursions to nowhere in particular. Walking baby around the block is fine, but here are some ideas on how to keep things moving and still get things done.

dancing baby

0–12 months

No, not that cute little graphic on the Internet that was so popular. Drs. William and Martha Sears recommend dancing with your baby as a way to soothe. Try the "Bounce," where baby, especially his head, is fully supported and held face-to-face while mom or dad bounces him *gently* but quickly up and down using arms or your legs. With the "Rock," move back and forth, bending at the waist. In the "Waltz," slide one foot forward, then slide the other foot forward to meet it. Personally, I always just stuck to back and forth!

moving attractions

sucking on the move

Sounds a little silly, but I became quite adept at breast-feeding while grocery shopping or doing almost anything. And my babies loved it. Something about being rocked a bit while they sucked quieted them right down, and there were days when I would not have managed to get out and about if I hadn't mastered this little trick. I accomplished this best by wearing a "nursing" blouse, with tactically placed slits, a cardigan sweater with a few of the buttons undone also works. I don't think anyone around me ever knew what I was doing. And I got arms of steel as I nursed with one arm and bent down to lift cans or laundry with the other.

moving attractions
on the ball

One woman swears by laying her baby over a flexible beach
ball or one of those giant Swiss exercise balls and rolling
him. Just lay baby (tummy down) over the ball and support
him as you slowly roll him
back and forth. Sounds
good for your back and
shoulders, too!

action humpty dumpty

6-12 months

Chant the popular nursery rhyme as you bounce your baby on your knees. "Humpty Dumpty sat on a wall..." (bounce baby); "Humpty Dumpty had a great fall..." (open your knees and, holding your baby securely, let him slide down to the ground); "All the kings horses and all the kings men couldn't put Humpty together again" (bring baby back to your knees). Once baby gets used to the rhythm, give him a favorite stuffed animal to hold as you play this game together. This may give him the idea to play the game with his stuffed animal, leaving you free to get on with something else.

drive,
just drive

0-12 months

Load up the car with troublesome package (i.e. crying baby),
pop in a CD (preferably something tranquil, not heavy
metal), and go for a ride. It rarely fails. Long or short, bumpy
road or not—a drive in the car, day or night, will definitely
calm a baby's frazzled nerves.

moving attractions

walk or hike

Walk or hike with baby in a front pack or sling or take her for walks around the neighborhood in her stroller. This way, you get out of the house and get some exercise while baby is soothed. But even at home, you'd be amazed at how much you can get done with baby in a sling. For years I couldn't afford one of the nicer slings so I made one out of a sturdy shawl. It worked perfectly and kept all of my babies peaceful while I did dishes or vacuumed the living room. Fortunately, the price of baby slings has come down in recent years, making them much more affordable, and you probably won't need to make your own!

jog or cycle

1-4 years

When she gets a bit older you can jog or cycle with your baby in a special jogging stroller or bike seat—but wait until she's at least six months old. Younger infants lack the neck strength to hold their heads upright and to support the weight of safety helmets. There are special jogging strollers on the market, but they are usually unsuitable for an older baby so may not be worth the investment.

moving attractions

0–12 months

road to nowhere

Where's that old treadmill or exercise bike you swore you'd work out on when the baby was born? Go drag it out of the garage because it's now or never. You can use them at anytime—including winter—and if baby is unhappy, you can put her in the front pack and walk nowhere with her as fast or slowly as you want.

exercise video

0–12 months

Use an exercise video at home with baby nearby. Just make sure she's safely napping or secure in an infant seat, highchair, or playpen, where she won't get underfoot. Chances are, she'll get a kick out of watching you dance! Be sure to stow potentially dangerous equipment out of her reach when you're done. If baby is old enough, get a video like "The Blue's Clues Musical" or "The Wiggles"

and design your own workout to fit the music of your baby's choice.

moving attractions

baby exercises

With exercises you can distract your baby and provide them with some entertainment. The double benefit is that you get to tone up and feel better about yourself at the same time. A couple of good exercises to do with a small (under six months) baby on your lap are:

The Baby Bridge: Lie on the floor with your knees bent and your feet flat on the floor. With baby on your lap, press your lower back to the floor and pull your navel to your spine (pelvic tilt). Then lift your buttocks off the floor and press your knees together squeezing the gluts (the buttock muscles) and inner thighs. Hold for five to 15 seconds, then repeat around ten times.

The Baby Curl: With baby on your lap, perform your sit-ups or crunches, saying "Boo" or something else silly when you make eye contact each time you come up.

Up, Up, and Away: Lie on your back on floor with your knees bent and baby lying on your chest face down. With your hands firmly under the baby's arms, lift him up in the air, then gently lower to your chest. Make a noise for takeoff and for landing.

other exercise to try

Flying Baby Curl: Lie on the floor on your back, with your feet and legs raised and your knees bent. With baby lying on his tummy on your shins, perform a curl, bringing your knees closer to your shoulders.

Semi-squats: Stand with legs apart, slightly wider than your shoulders (lean against a wall if you need more balance). Hold baby as you would normally, but in this case she will act as an extra weight, and gently squat halfway down. Baby will always enjoy added sound effects, and having a different view.

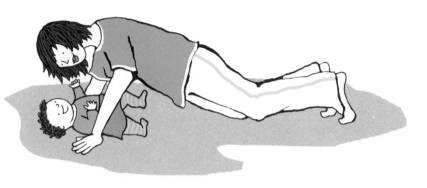

Kiss the Baby Push-ups: Start on your hands and knees, with baby on the floor between your hands. With your torso straight, hold your abs in tight as you bend your arms to lower your body toward the floor then straighten your arms to raise your body up. Kiss baby with each push-up.

lonesome tonight

Whether it's a blankie, a pacifier, or the front of mommy's sweater, babies and toddlers get attached to certain objects. These security objects are important—and although their company might at times be kind of embarrassing, you're not the only one to feel that way. Here are some tips on how to offer comfort and solace without tying yourself to the crib or the smelly blankie.

lonesome tonight?
decoy maneuver

0–12 months

One mom tells the story of finally getting her baby to sleep by nursing her and holding her. The only problem was, once baby fell asleep and mom tried to put her in her crib, she woke right up. There was just something about the smell of mom that baby couldn't sleep without. So, mom got smart and started putting a clean towel or T-shirt (depending on laundry availability!) between her and baby, and she developed a knack for slipping baby into bed, still clutching the towel.

lonesome tonight?

6 months–4 years

buy two

If junior's developed an affinity for a blanket or a certain stuffed animal, go and get another one. If it was a gift, ask the giver where it came from—they'll be so pleased that baby is that attached to their present that they won't mind disclosing the price. If you do this soon enough, baby will never know that his favorite stuffed puppy has a body double. This way, puppy #1 can be in the dryer while puppy #2 is still available for cuddles. Having a well-loved duplicate stashed in a safe place is also helpful if #1 gets lost or inadvertently left behind somewhere. You can limit the tears and heartbreak by explaining that puppy is simply waiting back at home.

honor thy blankie

lonesome tonight?

6 months–4 years

Life can be difficult when you aren't allowed to go out even to the mailbox without bringing blankie along. But there are ways to make bringing it along a little easier. One mom swears by making it smaller— especially if it's wearing out or your little one is going to playgroup or preschool. A square of a favorite blankie in a pocket can keep it hidden while it still works its magic.

lonesome tonight?

2-4 years

borrow it

Is your little one going out and it's just completely inappropriate to have a tattered, smelly, old blanket tagging along? Ask if you can borrow it for the day because you're feeling a little low. Most kids will readily understand and—as long as you promise to give it back—will give it up easily enough. Or suggest that teddy (or puppy or kitty or whatever stuffed toy is the current favorite) will be feeling a little bereft on his own for the day and that blanket would offer just the right kind of emotional comfort. If you do succeed in separating blanket from its proud owner, take advantage of the situation and give it a quick wash—I'm sure it could use one!

leaving in style

6 months–4 years

If your baby or toddler is finding it hard to deal with your leaving the house, leave the house together—parent, sitter, and baby. Go to the park or for a walk together. Separate from there, once baby is having fun, so that she doesn't have to watch you walk out of the door.

lonesome tonight?

6 months–4 years **build a team**

Spend time with other grown-ups. Get baby used to other people right from the beginning. The earlier you start leaving baby with other capable adults, even for very brief periods, the better off you will be later on. I didn't do this with my first and he screamed when I left him behind—even just to go to the bathroom. But I did do it with my daughter so she was used to hanging out with aunts and grandparents—and perfectly happy when I'd go away for a while! Very young babies usually settle pretty well with sitters, as long as they can be fed. This way, you can establish a habit before baby begins to experience stranger anxiety, at around the age of nine months or so.

play school

2-4 years

My kindergartener adjusted to leaving for school easily by playing school with her older sister and me the night before. By acting out what the day would bring and the different activities she would get to do, she was able to get excited about the day rather than feeling anxious.

lonesome tonight?

2-4 years

schedule it

It's up to you to stick to the plan. My child's preschool teacher warned me on the first day not to come early to pick him up (I desperately wanted to) because then my toddler would start expecting me at that time of the day every day. Make drop offs and pick ups at the same time each day (or as close as possible) and that way you won't be greeted by a little face pressed to the glass hoping mom will be back early. Kids quickly adapt to the routine of life in a preschool, and even though they can't tell time by the clock on the wall, they will know that mom will arrive a little after snack time or story time or whatever.

lonesome tonight?

virtual you

1-4 years

Going away on a trip? Or maybe even for a full day when you're usually only gone for a few hours? Record a couple of stories on a cassette tape and let baby or toddler (or even a school-aged child) hear your voice while you're gone. A picture of you will help your child feel like you're near and could be a comfort before bed or a nap.

lonesome tonight?

1-4 years

when you leave

The best way to establish confidence is to give a quick kiss and hug and then cheerfully say, "Good-bye." If you start to prolong your departure with extra hugs or leave and then come back several times this will only make the matter worse. And don't sneak out of the room. You are only delaying the moment of truth for your child. Be honest and be upfront. When it's time to go, it's time to go.

lonesome tonight?
new scary situations 2-4 years

Read a book, like Judith Viorst's *The Good Bye Book* (*see page 126* for other suggestions) and then have your child tell you a story, draw you a picture, or write you a story about what they think will happen while you are gone, or even what actually does happen when you leave. If they are in school or day care, maybe someone picks on them or there is a certain time of day they don't like. My own mother tells me how I hated going to a certain preschool. After talking with me about it a couple of days later, she discovered it wasn't separation anxiety at all. My mother was dropping me off in the middle of the day, which turned out to be naptime for all of the other kids, so I never wanted to go as I always felt the odd-one-out.

keeping your cool

Don't lose it. Take some time out for yourself. Being a parent is a full-time job, you are constantly in demand, and there's no union. So take a break, even if it means junior has to cry a little. You definitely deserve to do something for yourself sometimes. Here are some ways to take yourself safely out of the loop.

home work

0-4 years

Don't drown in boredom; your moods may affect your baby's. You're bored, he's bored. Don't (or can't) leave the baby, but want to do something besides fold yet another basketful of laundry? Teach yourself. There are courses that you can take on line or on cable TV. Go to the library and get an "Idiot's Guide" to almost any subject. I've seen guides for everything from Feng Shui and water gardening to yoga and, yup, even accounting!

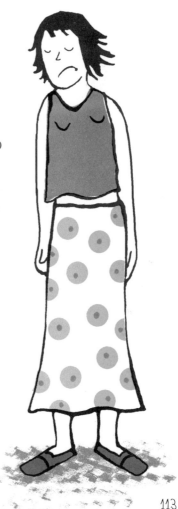

go away

Baby inconsolable? Feel like you're going to burst?

Put baby down. If you have done everything you can

think of and baby is still crying, don't let your frustration

grow. Put baby in his crib and close the door.

Take ten minutes and put on your

walkman, lie down, and listen

to music, or kick the

punching bag—whatever

it is that will help you

relieve stress. With any

luck, baby will have cried himself to sleep, and if not, then you'll be in a better position to deal with him. Encourage babysitters to do this as well. I always said, "I'd rather you put him down in his crib crying and walk away than get angry." How many shaken babies could have been saved if the caregiver wasn't frayed at the edges and took time out?

keeping your cool

1-4 years

go for a walk

Just go. Leave someone responsible with the baby, put on some sneakers, and walk out the door. It's so easy not to. It's so easy to be too tired. But you'll be amazed at how good you'll feel while you're out there, even if it's raining, and you'll feel even better when you get back, with a clear head.

eat well

1-4 years

It's tempting to finish the last bits of cereal or that last half a sandwich (although usually not the leftover strained carrots) and then forget to make yourself a meal. But do it. Make yourself a satisfying meal of your own choice, even if it's just PB&J or a salad, and sit down to eat it without rushing it. As a parent, you are busier than you have ever been, and you need to keep your strength up. It would be too easy to skip breakfast (and lunch) and then pig out before bed once baby is asleep. This isn't just upsetting for your tummy, it's unhealthy and piles the pounds on. Make a point of having three balanced meals a day, and you'll feel— and look—better for it.

get plenty of sleep

0-4 years

Alternate with your partner on the weekends as to who gets up early with the kids. Its amazing how rejuvenating it can be to have even just a few extra minutes in bed on your own. Add a leisurely shower and we're talking bliss.

a special place, just for you

0-4 years

Make a special place just for you. The kids have the playroom and the jungle gym out back. Dad might have an office (to go to, or in the house) and maybe the garage or basement and mom has . . . the kitchen? I think not. Find a big, overstuffed chair—yard sales are great for this—and a great reading lamp and make a cozy place to read. Or create a little escape in your garden: lawn chair or chaise, side table and a nice big glass of, shall we say, lemonade.

Let the kids play while you, well, don't. Let everyone know that your time in your chair is sacrosanct. For ten minutes, the kids can play on their own and requests for snacks can go unanswered.

long term
strategies

When baby is old enough to be left with a caregiver and you can surface for air, build in some downtime for yourself in your weekly routine. It is so important to get to talk to other grown-ups on a regular basis, particularly without the kids around. Join a book club, take a class, volunteer for something in the neighborhood, book a night out with your single pals, or organize a regular Mom's Night Out with other women you know who are in the same boat. That sweet little face you left sleeping in your spot in bed looks even more precious after you've been away—even if it's only for a couple of hours.

growl but don't scream 2-4 years

One dad swears that acting like a big, growling bear instead of yelling. "Who's been pouring sugar on the kitchen floor?" is a much more controlled (and yet still firm) response than hollering about the mess. It also adds a little humor to the situation, without being intimidating. After all, we just want them to not to pour sugar on the floor on purpose— not be scared of us permanently.

GRUrrr

do over!

Did you ever shout that as a kid? It's a "Do over!" Try one now, as a grown-up. Take a breath, walk around a bit, and then reapproach the situation. "Let's try this again," I often say this when I realize my yelling has become incoherent and out of control. "Now, just how did the gum get stuck to the dog?" When tempers get frayed, we all need time-outs—not just mom and dad but the little ones, too. So go for some enforced quiet time, with everyone sitting—more than arm's length apart—and flipping through a book or magazine or playing with a doll or a toy car. Even just five minutes of relative calm will create a better atmosphere. Then you can all try a do over.

take a lap

1-4 years

Is everyone on each other's nerves? If the kids are old enough, make 'em run a lap around the house with you (or the yard, or block, heck even the park if you have to). What first seemed like punishment can quickly turn into a fun-run for the last popsicle in the freezer. Often a lack of exercise causes a build-up of kid energy. So go for a run. The kids get their release and you'll be panting too hard to yell at them!

0-4 years **call your mother**

The bathtub is overflowing, the baby is screaming "MOMMY!", the phone is ringing, there's a kid at the door trying to sell you a magazine subscription, and you just stepped on another Lego. It's all you can do to keep from screaming yourself. The best call I can ever make at times like these is to call my mom and tell her about all of the horrible things my children are doing and then listen while she bursts out laughing. Because undoubtedly this call is affirmation that the curse worked. Ah yes, the curse your own mother put on you—that you might have children who behaved just as you did. Well, take heart! After you have vented (and told your mother to stop laughing), you can retrieve the curse from her and put it on your kids. If you're not in the mood for mom (or couldn't get her to stop laughing), call a good friend, preferably one with children or one who admires your childrearing abilities (not the one that thinks you're crazy for having for kids). Whoever you call, choose someone who will let you rant and rave for five minutes and who will help you see the funny side of it all. Believe it or not, there usually is one.

further reading

GACH, MICHAEL REED.
Acupressure's Potent Points: A Guide to Self-Care for Common Ailments.
New York: Bantam Doubleday Dell Publishers, 1990.

HINES, ANNA GROSSNICKLE.
Even if I Spill my Milk?
New York: Clarion Books, 1994.

JARMEY, CHRIS.
Acupressure for Common Ailments.
Columbus, Ohio: Fireside, 1991.

TEEGUARDEN, IONA M. & TEEGUARD, IONA
Acupressure Way of Health Jin Shin Do.
Tokyo: Japan Publishers, 1978.

VIORST, JUDITH.
The Good-bye Book.
New York: Atheneum, 1998.

WELLS, ROSEMARY.
Mama, Don't Go!
New York: Hyperion Press, 2001.

notes

diagnostic clues

1 Your baby does not feed as well as normal. The baby may not seem hungry and may not take as much of the feeding as normal.

2 Your baby vomits with force all or most of the feeding.

3 Your baby has frequent, watery stools (has more stools than usual and they are very watery). Babies usually have bowel movements that are formed and yellow to brown color and they have a bowel movement after feedings or every day or two.

4 Your baby does not pass as much urine as usual (fewer wet diapers). Usually babies wet their diapers almost hourly.

5 Your baby refuses to sleep.

6 Your baby does not seem as active as usual.

7 Your baby may be difficult to wake from sleep.

8 Your baby may have trouble breathing or breathes faster and harder and may draw in chest muscles with each breath or may have noisy breathing.

9 Your baby may have a fever. Contact the doctor if temperature is 100°F or higher.

10 Your baby's color may appear pale, bluish, or marbled-looking. A sunken or bulging fontanel (soft spot) is an immediate need for attention.

index

Acknowledgments

I would like to thank my children, my husband, Rebecca Saraceno, and Mandy Greenfield.